Motivated Muslimah: Permission to Win

Copyright © 2017 by Walida Muhammad This book was printed in the United States of America. ISBN: 9781941919026 All rights reserved. No part of this book may be reproduced or transmitted in any form or by any means, electronic or mechanical, including photocopying, recording, or by+ any information storage and retrieval system, without permission in writing from the copyright owner. Printed in the United States of America

Table of Contents

Inspiration 4 You!...4

8 Quick Steps to Start Reclaiming Your Life 5

Introduction 6

Chapter 1- Believing that Allah is sufficient for all of your needs.. 10

Chapter 2- She strives to pray more than the 5 daily prayers 17

Chapter 3- Her hereafter is worth more than her dunya (life)... 24

Chapter 4- Striving for excellence, not perfection, in all things good... 31

Chapter 5-Being proactive.. 39

Chapter 6-Failing with grace- Knowing that Allah is in control 43

Chapter 7- Not the "Asiyyah of all trades" 51

Chapter 8- Saying "NO" with humble confidence......... 55

Chapter 9- She consistently seeks to get out of her own way when embarking on her goal. 62

Chapter 10-She trains her subconscious mind 67

Chapter 11-Taking 100% Responsibility for your life- . 82

Chapter 12-Treating the Body as an Amanah(trust from Allah) 99

Inspiration 4 You!

Change is not easy but staying in the same circumstance that has been mentally and physically draining you is way more difficult! Start doing that thing you fear and become that person you want to become and change happens automatically!- Ukhtee Walida-The Boss Moms Coach

It has been reported that, The Prophet Muhammad, peace and blessings be upon him, said: "Whoever Allah wants good for, He puts them to test. He puts them through difficulties; like a diamond or gold that has to be burnt after which anything bad from it is removed so that what you have is the pure diamond or the pure gold." (Bukhari Muslim)

"A quitter never wins-and-a winner never quits."
― Napoleon Hill, Author of "Think and Grow Rich"

"Trust yourself. Think for yourself. Act for yourself. Speak for yourself. Be yourself. Imitation is suicide." – Marva Collins

"Mostly, the world sees you the way you see yourself."
― Lisa Nichols, "No Matter What!: 9 Steps to Living the Life You Love"

8 Quick Steps to Start Reclaiming Your Life

1. Press Reset!
2. Find a quiet spot and begin to Breathe(focused, still, and slowly)
3. State at least 7 affirmations one after another (positive statements about yourself and what you want to attract in your life) ex. (say "In the name of God" before stating your affirmations) I am beautiful, I am brilliant, I am amazing, etc...
4. Ask yourself "What do I want to happen in my life? Why do I want this? What price am I paying for not making it happen?
5. Forgive yourself and anyone else who you feel was in the way of you having a great life(your life is only 10% what happens to you and 90% how you react to what happens)
6. Write down at least 3 SMART goals you want to accomplish in the next 3 - 6 months Create an Actionable Road Map
7. Get Support (hire a coach, gather a team, friends, others who have achieved what your trying to achieve etc...)
8. Take Action Like your life depends on it!

Introduction

As Salaamu Alaykum(may peace be upon you) and Great Day beloveds! Before I get to what I want to say to you let me start by letting you know a little bit about me and my journey from where I came to where I am going. I was born, Walida Muhammad, in Long Island, New York. I was raised as a Muslim and so that is my foundation and what I will always live as, God Willing, until the day my soul returns to Allah. If you are not Muslim and you are about to read this book I figured that you should know I am the kind of Muslim that wants you to know about me and ask questions so that you don't have to figure anything out or assume. For starters, I pray five times a day to Allah (God) facing the direction of the Kaaba in Mecca as all Muslims around the world must do. I pray for peace, happiness, prosperity, and patience and strength through hardships just like you! This book was not written for you to judge whether I am holy enough or to even think you cannot benefit from it because you are not Muslim. It is from the perspective of a Muslim girl who just wanted to finally get into a space of empowerment and motivation after enduring sexual abuse in her childhood and emotional abuse in her adulthood and just fed up feeling unworthy, hopeless, ugly and unmotivated. I just knew that my life was supposed to be great! I laugh because I know you are not caring about all of this but you are looking for something that speaks to your struggles and I must say it can speak to you if you take a moment to just open your mind and heart and peel back your tough skin for about 7 days. That's how long I think it will take you to read and do all of the activities within this book. I think you and I are human and that is more than enough reason for you to find some benefit in this book if you are feeling stuck and unmotivated day in and day out as you strive to achieve long awaited goals.

I am a survivor and a victor not a victim of what has happened to me in my past and the same goes for you too my dear friend. I just cannot allow my pain to consume me and be the air that I breathe daily and neither should you. I needed to know that I am phenomenal, beautiful, funny, kind, smart, successful, relentless, compassionate, and can make a powerful impact on others so I decided to go on this journey to arrive at a place of peace and motivation on purpose to make my life happen on terms that I have set instead of letting others and circumstances define me. I validate me first! Besides I am the only one who can decide how I want my life to be and have no one to blame for it except myself if I allow others and circumstances to ruin it! I am still healing today.

Now some things may have happened to you either similarly or different and you are still struggling to just get over them already but cannot just drop it and move on. I was just where you are and not too long ago! If you want to reclaim your energy and your life and begin operating at your best then you have stepped into the right book. If you're willing, I'd like to take you on my own journey of self-motivation and help you focus on areas of yourself that you have been pushing underneath the rug for fear that it would make you get real with yourself and cause norm disruption. Well they say "if nothing changes then nothing changes. Now if you are ready read the following...

Today I want you to think about where you stand and how far you have become. Don't worry yourself with what went wrong and who wronged you, just simply breathe and get ready to embrace who you truly are and prepare yourself to enjoy the journey to where you want to be. It's time you let go of those lies you have been telling yourself about why your life is the way it is and dig deep down inside to surface the goodness in you. I know how hard it is to do this because it personally took me a decade and a half to show up in my own life as my authentic self. I can't tell you how amazing this transformation has been since I decided to accept me for me and to choose to impact the lives of women just like you!

You have the awesome power of resilience that was given to you in your mother's womb and there is no time better than NOW to act on it. You just have to believe that your life is supposed to be about serving and that it is not only about YOU and what YOU could get! Serving Allah(God) first and serving His creation with the gifts that He has created you with, guarantees reward from Him and we know His bounties are endless. I want to motivate and empower you to find your gifts and eventually deliver them, by Allah's permission, because I believe in YOU! I am your "sister and I am committed to helping you get real with yourself and the circumstances that have been surrounding your life. I am addicted to helping women like you make a serious shift towards a life of winning! You win and I win so nobody is losing!

Let's do this! Fail Forward! I want you to "Start Where You Are and Finish Where You Want to Be"! Coach Ukhtee Walida- The Boss Moms Coach

1- Believing that Allah is sufficient for all of your needs

"Allah says, 'I am as my servant expects me to be, and I am with him when he remembers me. If he thinks of Me, I think of him. If he mentions me in company, I mention him in an even better company. When he comes closer to me by a hand span, I come closer to him by an arm's length. If he draws closer to me by an arm's length, I draw closer by a distance of two outstretched arms, nearer to him. If my servant comes to me walking, I go to him running." *(Source: Ṣaḥīḥ al-Bukhārī 6970)*

You must not be afraid to walk away from toxic or harmful relationships and situations. Know that your Lord is sufficient for all your needs. I encourage you to call on Allah much in your days of prosperity and call on Him in adversity with patience.

To give you an example of this, think about situations where people are suffering in toxic Relationships and stay because they fear the loss of something or someone. They truly are doing themselves a disservice. They pay a high price for convincing themselves that their patience and hope alone will put everything back in place! The raw truth is that if this is your story; know that staying in an unhealthy relationship or situation can be quite detrimental. The harmful effect of becoming severely depressed alone has real consequences, let alone the effects of feeling trapped in a harmful relationship.

Some of us will stay with a dead end job because we believe it is the only way to make ends meet. Others actually get a divorce, hoping for the misery to disappear, only to find their own thoughts and beliefs wreaking havoc in their lives. For example, they fear that they are not worthy of marriage, or if they re-marry, their next husband would be worse. Similarly, one could also relent to develop a business venture as a result of being discouraged from past attempts that were deemed unprofitable. The answer may not be in leaving, but it may be in something we most often overlook.

Whatever your fears are about what you can have, do, or achieve can be fixed by strengthening your relationship with The One who created you. After all, He is The One who fashioned you and has written your fate. So why stress yourself out about how to get through these struggles, when, without a doubt, Allah can relieve you of them and grant you better? Now, don't be fooled into thinking that du'a devoid of action or sincere effort to put forth effort is plausible. Choosing to idly exist in those toxic situations will beget years of more suffering until and unless you decide to do something different. You must put forth the necessary effort to bring about your desired results while asking Allah to grant you relief.

I recommend that you master the art of asking. How do you do this? It sounds simple but it takes work. It involves asking from Allah with trust that you will get what you asked for and exert the effort. Simply put, the motivated Muslimah who gives herself permission to win, knows that du'a(prayer) is powerful. She knows that Allah is as she thinks of him so she makes du'a as if he will grant her what she asks of him and does her best not to doubt or despair when the road gets tough. She knows that the speed bumps along her journey are there for her to make a better come-back and strive harder. She knows that her success in this life cannot happen alone, and that she must seek Allah's help in all that she hopes to achieve. She knows that Allah will give to her from places she cannot even imagine and that she should not worry about the source of her blessings. She must be grateful and ready to receive the blessings from Allah!

What can appear to be bizarre but true is that within your storms of difficulty, you will find ease if you truly believe in and seek from the Creator? People are not guarantors of relief because they are not the owners of it. It is through others that Allah may send you help but they are not the source of it. If an affliction or adversity befalls you, then know that it was written for you and if it did not befall you, then it was not written for you.

Allah sends hardships and trials to those whom He loves.

When I sat down to write this book, I had recently began studying the first ten ayaats of Surah Al Kahf and I have never been so engulfed in learning the Quran as I am now. Reading Allah's words in the Arabic language and looking up the transliterated meaning of the words in my Hans Wehr Arabic English dictionary has given me a much better understanding of the messages from Creator. Never have I been able to gain half as much understanding reading the Qur'an in English, my native tongue.

A major tool in helping me grasp meaning of Allah's powerful and potent words have been an invaluable website created by Nouman Ali Kahn at www.bayyinahtv.com. This resource is packed with material needed for an in depth study of Quranic Arabic. It has really opened up so many opportunities for me, including this very book that I am writing now! In addition, it has assisted to mend the relationship between me and my children, facilitated me in learning more of the Deen(religion) on a consistent basis, and making new strides in my business, just to name a few!

What led me to all of this is a class that I had been taking with an instructor who really pushes his students to learn to read and understand the Quran in the language in which it was sent, Arabic. I have learned through these few ayaats the beauty of how these young men fled for refuge to the cave and made it their utmost priority, despite the hardship they endured as the boulder closed them into the cave, to call upon Allah for relief. The lesson I learned from reading, reciting, and finding meaning to these ten ayaat was that we should make it our number one priority to call on Allah much, thank him often and we will find him near when we are in desperate need of reprieve.

Abu al-'Abbas 'Abdullah bin 'Abbas(may Allah be pleased with him) reports:

> "One day I was riding (a horse/camel) behind the Prophet, peace and blessings be upon him, when he said, 'Young man, I will teach you some words. Be mindful of God, and He will take care of you. Be mindful of Him, and you

shall find Him at your side. If you ask, ask of God. If you need help, seek it from God. Know that if the whole world were to gather together in order to help you; they would not be able to help you except if God had written so. And if the whole world were to gather together in order to harm you; they would not harm you except if God had written so. The pens have been lifted, and the pages are dry.' " *(40 hadith an nawawi, 2017:Hadith No. 19) Related by At-Tirmidthi)*

Time for A.C.T.I.O.N.

Set your timer for 15 minutes.

Grab a pen and write down some things that have been troubling you in at least one area of your life. Ask yourself these questions.

Have I asked for Allah's help with this? If no, why not? What did it cost me to hold back from seeking aid with Allah?

_____
_____
_____
_____
_____
_____
_____
_____

_____
_____
_____
_____
_____
_____
_____
_____
_____
_____

_____

May Allah guide you to seek only from Him in your darkest moments and remember him much in prosperity. Ameen!

> *Chapter 2- She strives to pray more than the 5 daily prayers*

The Muslim woman is obliged to pray the 5 obligatory prayers but she can also pray extra prayers in her striving to get closer to Allah. She may pray Sunnah prayers, prayers that were done by the Prophet Muhammad (May peace and blessings be upon him) and may also pray nafl (extra) prayers in her attempt to gain the pleasure of Allah. The best description of the believing woman who reaches the level of drawing closer to Allah by consistently doing good, extra deeds can be seen in the following Hadith Qudsi:

"My servant continues to draw near to Me with supererogatory works so that I will love him. When I love him, I am his hearing with which he hears, his seeing with which he sees, his hand with which he strikes, and his foot with which he walks. Were he to ask [something] of Me, I would surely give it to him; and were he to ask Me for refuge, I would surely grant him it." *(40 hadith Qudsi,:Hadith No. 25)Related by Al-Bukhari)*

Praying Qiyam ul Layl opens up so many blessings for the believer. A Muslimah benefits greatly when she strives to pray to Allah while the night is still and others are resting. She seeks to strengthen her connection with Allah by seeking His forgiveness, mercy and reward. The following are a few ahadith concerning the benefits of Qiyyam ul Layl.

Hadith Qudsi 35:

On the authority of Abu Hurayrah (may Allah be pleased with him), who said that the Messenger of Allah (PBUH) said: Our Lord (glorified and exalted be He) descends each night to the earth's sky when there remains the final third of the night, and He says: Who is saying a prayer to Me that I may answer it? Who is asking something of Me that I may give it him? Who is asking forgiveness of Me that I may forgive him?

(40 Hadith Qudsi,:Hadith No. 35) Related by Muslim, Malik, At-Tirmidthi and Abu Dawud)

Jabir (may Allah be pleased with him) reported that he heard the Messenger of Allah, may peace and blessings be upon him, saying, "There is an hour in the night in which no Muslim servant will implore Allah for good in this world and the next without Allah giving it to him, and that applies to every night." *(Sahih Muslim Book 4, No. 1654)*

He (may peace and blessings be upon him) said: "You should pray Qiyaam al-Layl, for it is the habit of the righteous people who came before you, and it will bring you closer to your Lord, expiate for bad deeds, prevent sin, and expel disease from the body." *[Narrated by At-Tirmidhee and Musnad Ahmad]*

While you strive to meet your goals it will serve you best if you preceded all acts with Ibadah (worship). Remember nothing will happen without Allah's will. Qiyam al Layl keeps your eeman (faith) renewed and increases it. So many blessings open up during those most precious hours of the night. Allah comes to the lowest part of the heavens and literally grants forgiveness, mercy and whatever else we ask of Him. Some believers who pray Qiyyam ul Layl begin to experience changes in their lives almost immediately. Before they started performing Qiyyam ul Layl they were feeling confused about making decisions that were important to their personal, family, and business lives. They needed clarity and they also wanted to receive Allah's bounties, so the sacrifice was worth it for them!

A highly productive and striving Muslimah often checks her intentions for the goals she wants to achieve because her ultimate aim is to please Allah in all that she seeks. She wants nothing more than to have her deeds accepted by Allah. She believes that her success is not attained truly unless her striving for it was for the sake of attaining mercy from her Lord. She conducts a self-analysis to check her intentions by examining her relationships with her family, friends, co-workers, business partners and people in her community. Next to the relationship with Allah and His Prophet (May peace be upon him) which is first and foremost, the relationship with her family is of utmost importance. The obedience that one must give to the parents is the first relationship that must be cultivated and respected. Allah positioned the obedience to parents' right after obedience to Him and one can see this in Quran as Allah says:

دَيْنِاِحْسَـٰنًا۞وَقَضَىرَبُّكَأَلاَّتَعْبُدُواْإِلاَّإِيَّـهُوَبِالْوَل

"Your Lord has decreed that you worship none but Him, and that you be dutiful to your parents." *(The Noble Quran 17:23)*

In another surah Allah says:

أَنِاشْكُرْلِىوَلِوَلِدَيْكَإِلَىَّالْمَصِيرُ

Be grateful to Me and to your parents. Unto Me is the final destination. *(The Noble Quran 31:14)*

It is my hope that you understand, more than before, that the habit of constantly making du'a to Allah is a treasure, when we are deep in our trials and are looking for a clear way out! We want the adversity removed swiftly but rarely accept it. Accept adversity? Who wants to do that anyway? Accepting the challenges of adversity can be quite painful but until we do, the tunnel shows no light. You may be lifted from the suffering but the core of the adversity still exists and may return with a different picture. Have you ever been in a situation that makes you feel like you have been there before?

Time for A.C.T.I.O.N.

This will be easy if you know a couple of du'as already!

Grab a pen

Set your timer for 15 minutes, no longer than 25! You don't want to become frustrated at all because it will ruin the process!

Begin to write down a du'a that you would feel is most befitting for a trying situation you are enduring right now. Leave some space before the du'a and some space after. (Feel free to use the space below)

What is going on right now that I am either worried about or am dissatisfied about?

_____

_____

_____
_____
_____

Why am I dissatisfied or worried about this?

_____
_____
_____
_____
_____

What can I do to shift my negative emotions about this to ones that are more desirable and positive?

_____
_____
_____
_____
_____
_____
_____

What have a tried so far? What has worked and what has not?

_____
_____
_____
_____

_____
_____
_____

Write a dua that relates to your situation. Example: Dua for relieving anxiety. Write what you want from Allah concerning the situation. Be very specific!

_____
_____
_____
_____
_____
_____
_____
_____
___

Put forth an effort by writing a plan of how you will work to shift your emotion about the situation!

_____
_____
_____
_____
_____
_____
_____

Try making your best to say this dua daily however often as you like! Record what your attitude is about the situation as the days go by. I recommend keeping a journal close by to record your progress, setbacks, and success. Don't struggle with this activity; enjoy the process of it. Laugh at yourself and cry if you need to but Don't Give In to the SHAYTAAN suggesting that you might as well just remain miserable. Pick yourself up with the dua you wrote when you begin to feel like nothing is working for you! Feel free to send me an email about your journey!

I'd love to hear all about it!
mmpermission2win@gmail.com

May Allah bestow mercy upon you from Himself and may He dispose of your affairs in the right way. Ameen!

Chapter 3- Her hereafter is worth more than her dunya (life).

"Did you then think that we have created you in jest and that you would not be brought back to us (for account)"? *(The Noble Quran 23:115)*

She desires the hereafter and strives for it in an attempt to achieve goals in the dunya. The motivated Muslimah gives herself permission to live by not living for this life because she knows that it is only temporary; her length of time here will end and is only known by Allah. She seeks to do as many righteous deeds and performs as much ibadah (worship for Allah) as she can while living in this life. One thing that she really seeks to understand is her purpose in this life. She knows that the first purpose of life for all human beings is to worship Allah so she designs a life that will incorporate her worship making for a very wholesome and fulfilling life. It is true that she may get attached to the things of this temporal world but this is her struggle to connect with her Lord and she will be judged by her intention of all of it. What seems like such a regret can be Allah's way of calling her to get closer to Him. She can receive many blessings by being patient when struck with adversity instead of giving up trust and hope in Allah. She knows that being patient is the first test so she strives to attain this level of patience though it can be very tough to attain. She only wants from this life what will bring her closer to her Lord and His ajr (reward) of the hereafter.

In Islam, Muslims are taught that striving solely for this world will leave them in much distress and cause them to be losers in the next life. Furthermore, when you put this dunya (this life) in your heart, it is almost like getting tricked by a "wolf dressed in sheep clothing"! Anyone who is deceived by its beauty and glamour is at a terrible loss! Constant distress, worry and unhappiness tend to be the "roller coaster" being ridden daily. Chasing money, fame and love only fills their feeling of void long enough to satisfy them in "the moment." It is a perpetual thought in their minds that they are not and cannot be successful without these things.

What does it mean to the Muslim woman? I will tell you that we are human and desire things that we feel will make us satisfied in life just like anyone else. Being distressed and worrying about not having money is also normal. We all have different levels of tolerance. One woman may be able to tolerate not having money while another may feel like she is totally losing her mind without it. What holds us together is constant reminders of Allah's bounties, putting our trust in Allah, and being productive for the sake of Allah. We believe that our source of provision is solely from Allah and we know that in order to become successful in this life, and in the next, we must be consistent in our worship to Him.

Contrary to what many believe, women are a major asset to society even given their classification as the "rib". Females were created as help mates to men; we obey them and support them in their efforts. Allah says, in the interpretation of the meaning of the Qur'an: O mankind! Fear your Lord who created you from a single soul and of like nature his mate and from the two scattered [like seeds] countless men and women. *(The Noble Quran 4:1)*

The ribs are an important part of our bodies. If we were to think of women as such, we would know that the function of the ribs is to protect the heart and the lungs from damage and to give assistance to the lungs for the purposes of breathing. Now I like to think of us as being soft with our husbands similar to protection of the heart and lungs. The support we give our husbands in their efforts is like the assistance that the ribs give to the lungs for the purpose of breathing.

Have you ever experienced the smile on your husband's face when he is just so content with you for being who you are? When he comes through the door with a face that, if looks could kill, you would be dead! Then because you have dressed yourself in the finest clothing, have the sweetest smelling oil all over you, walk towards him with a smile, and slowly lean over to give him the most luscious kiss ever he suddenly turns into a soft cuddly bear! You may prepare him some tea and something light to snack on while you run the bath water infused with jasmine Epsom salt and a little bit of bubbles. Once you have done that you may remove his socks and massage his feet before he gets into the bathtub. Trust me! Your husband will have no choice but to love you just for that act alone! Asking him how his day went could be good or bad depending on when you ask. If he is too irate then asking him will only make his day worse especially if you have to tell him the truth about how he may have handled something. I mean, you may be right but that could start a fire, if you know what I mean! Wait until you have fed him and he is relaxed. And when you ask, starting with a nick-name you have for him or something sweet sounding may be in your best favor. Calling him by his name may make it sound like you are not really interested in knowing about his feelings. It sounds strange but think of it in this way; if your mother called you by your whole name it usually meant you were either going to get admonished or she needed you to do something, however if she calls you by that special nick-name she has given you since birth it softens you up and you readily accept her request. She may be calling you to compliment you on how well you are doing at school or just to give you a hug!

My point in all of this is that you have been created from the nature of Adam to be his mate and helper, and the society in which we live in today in America, has suggested that women are like men and can do better than men so long as they become independent of men. The message is subliminal and our children are subjected to this message when they turn on the television day after day. They rarely get to see the woman in her most powerful position, THE HOME! They often have to see the husband and wife as rivals with each other and competing instead of compromising and supporting one another's roles. Alhamdulilah (All praise is due to Allah)! Allah created us women in such an amazing fashion and highly respected status.

So with that said, wouldn't you agree that we have a special place in society and a large portion of that relies heavily on the upbringing of our children? We must understand that the successful upbringing of a nation that has good morals and principles begins with our striving to please Allah in regards to ourselves, husbands, children, families and communities. We have to display marriage correctly to our children otherwise the divorce rate will remain high and the cycle of dysfunction will continue to be prevalent in our ummah (community). We must be aware that we will only live until an appointed term, of which we have absolutely no knowledge of. Worshipping Allah in all that we do in this life is what we must find ourselves attracted to as vicegerents on the Earth if we want to be successful.

The motivated Muslimah should race to do her best in this life (deeds, actions etc...) for the sake of The One (Allah) who created her and will reward her for doing so.

Time for A.C.T.I.O.N!

Grab a pen and a sheet of paper!

Set your timer for about 10minutes.

Write down a list of actions that you partake in, regarding your business, that reflect your conscious about Allah being the source of your provision and success in this life and in the hereafter. Keep this list in your planner or hang it on a wall in your office to be reminded about it often. You will want to do these actions often.

Chapter 4- Striving for excellence, not perfection, in all things good

One of the words for effort in Arabic is jahada. It means exertion, endeavor, attempt, effort etc... One (of) the words for excellence in Arabic is Ihsan. It means blameless, unblemished reputation, integrity etc... Why am I giving you the definition to these words? Well what you are about to read has much to do with these words and their meaning in English is very limited. We should strive for excellence in all things. We don't want to just settle for completion or kill ourselves over perfection. Excellence means putting forth effort with integrity. Give it all you got! You don't have to obsess over anything because your best is your best and that is enough! When we start doubting ourselves and feeling uneasy it is only the shaytaan that has whispered this to us. It sounds like you're thinking these thoughts all alone or it's a figment of your imagination but the reality is that he does this when you make statements like "if only I had done... or "if I could ... etc. He works day and night to cause scruples in your subconscious and awaken your doubts leaving you paralyzed at the thought that what you have done is not good enough. I encourage you to seek protection with Allah from him as much as you can so that you can avert his evil influence.

"And if an evil whisper comes to you from Shaitan (Satan) then seek refuge with Allah. Verily, He is All-Hearer, All-Knower.

Say "Authoo Billahi Mina Shaytaa Nir Rajeem"- I seek refuge with Allah from shaytaan the accursed one. *(The Noble Qur'an -Surah Al Araf:200)*

Abu Saeed al-Khudri said: "The Messenger of Allah (may peace and blessings be upon him) used to seek refuge with Allah from the jinn and from the evil eye until the Mu'wadaitain were revealed, and when they were revealed he started to recite them and not anything else" *(narrated by al-Tirmidhi, 2058; he said it is hasan ghareeb). Also narrated by al-Nasaa'i, 5494; Ibn Maajah, 3511).*

The two surahs mentioned in this hadith are Surah Al- Falaq and Surah-An Nas.

When we strive to do good things in this life it gives us the opportunity to receive Allah's Mercy and reward. The Prophet, may peace and blessings be upon him, said "Allah has prescribed Al Ihsan in every matter". *(Sahih Muslim)*

Umar ibn Al-Khattab reported: The Messenger of Allah, peace and blessings be upon him, said: Excellence is to worship Allah as if you see Him, for although you do not see Him yet He certainly sees you. *(Sahih Muslim)*

We are encouraged to strive with integrity in our relationship with Allah, ourselves, and others. This can be very difficult at times because we live in a society that demands us to compete, compete, compete and be perfect, whether it be with others or ourselves. We are forced to socialize and live in an environment that constantly threatens our opportunities for personal improvement. The need to be the best is within all of us but it can become stressful. We sometimes get paralyzed at analyzing how we will complete a task because we are so worried about it not coming out right. It nearly drives us crazy and we may even become stressed or just shut down from the world. It's mostly fear of failure in one of its many masked forms. You begin striving for perfection and getting half done or nothing done instead of striving for excellence. You can't seem to do your utmost best and be satisfied with it.

I definitely can identify with this thing called striving for perfection. Many people, including myself, have struggled at one time or another trying to perfect something. While I was writing this book I would often get writer's "block" and just get frustrated because my mind would not allow the words to flow to my pen. I would stop for days and even months because I just did not feel it would be good enough. I knew that this book would just be in my brain for the rest of my life and that I could be dying with something that may benefit others. I felt so terrible. I had told so many people that the book was coming out soon but I fell into a depressed mode since I was in an unhappy marriage and this is what caused my block. Little did I know that this chapter of my life would finally come to an end so that I could get to know myself again. I know it may seem like this has nothing to do with striving for excellence but it truly does. I was at a low point and because of it I had used it as an excuse to overanalyze my ability to finish what I had started. I began to think" no one is going to want to read this" and "there are more qualified authors who could do a better job than I ". Shaytaan was having such a ball with me! He awakened my doubts and just continued to suggest that I should be worried about the perfection in what I was going to write. This made me procrastinate and it was not a good feeling but I was afraid of going forward anymore with it. I had just gotten in my own way of achieving my goal to write the book at this point. I would not let anyone encourage me to finish this book. I had a firm wall up and just gave up!

During the Fall of 2014, it had been two years since I visited my original manuscript. I realized something needed to change. The divorce was certainly a major life altering event but I was going to use my energy in more positive ways to get past my emotions about it. I had to be grateful to Allah for my marriage and for my divorce if I wanted to move forward! Losing was not an option anymore! I had to give myself permission to win. I immediately decided that I will not give up! I knew that I had to put my trust in Allah even more now, so I began making dua and started to roll my sleeves up!

I had to unleash my potential once again! I had to stop living in my past and begin living in the present and hoping for a brighter future! I began to write my plans for completing my book and realized that I had no one to support me and guide me in my endeavor. I looked up a list of people that I knew who were authors and came across a good friend of mine. Her name is Subhanah Wahhaj Author of "How I Found Myself in Egypt". She had recently started a publishing company called "The Write Patch". We spent about an hour on the phone while I discussed my book and I hired her the same day as my writing coach and got started right away! Yes even coaches need coaching! I had known how successful she was as an author and I thought that it would be to my advantage to hire her as a writing coach. I could not have done it without

Allah putting her in my path and helping as much as she did. She encouraged me when I did not want to encouraged, she never criticized me for wanting to just give up but she would suggest that I take a break here and there to release stress. She showed me how to enjoy the process of completing my book instead of dreading it. I decided that striving for excellence was exactly what I was doing. This was it! I could no longer just complete my book or drive myself crazy over it being perfect. I had begun a revolution with my thoughts. My thoughts and speech had to improve too so that I could give myself the permission to win. I no longer wanted to stand in my way.

Time for A.C.T.I.O.N.

Set your timer for 15 minutes and do this activity below!

Some of the following symptoms of perfection are below. I am very familiar with a few. How many resonate with you? Put a check mark next (to) them. Ask yourself what it is costing you to behave like this and what are you going to do about it.

- Do you have extremely high expectations for yourself?

- Do you have to excel at every task you perform otherwise you feel like a failure or a loser?

- Do you feel a sense of failure when you don't achieve the goal you had set for yourself?

- Do people around you feel as if they can never meet your expectations?

- Are you motivated by fear of failure rather than the possibility of truly becoming successful?

- Do you look down on your own worth in regards to your achievements?

- Do you have the 'all' or 'nothing' attitude when assessing your progress?

- Are you reluctant to accepting compliments even when you have been successful?

- Do you procrastinate on projects that others will have to give an opinion about?

- Do you repeatedly start over on projects or take a long time to just get started?

- Are you a person who is reluctant to readily answer questions making sure that your answer is correct before speaking?(always on the defense)

- Are you highly emotional to minor failures or disappointments?(small setbacks)

- Must you achieve everything perfectly/flawless?

May Allah protect you from shaytaan's evil suggestions that awaken your doubts and cause confusion in your conscience and guide you to strive with excellence instead of perfection- Ameen!

Chapter 5 - Being proactive

The Prophet, peace and blessings be upon him, said:

"The religion is easy and whosoever will deal with religion harshly, it will defeat him. So be straight, follow the middle course, give good news and make use of the morning, the evening or part of the night (in prayer and remembering Allah)." *(Sahih Al-Bukhari)*

Are you a reactive or proactive person? Let me give you a brief background of both. To be reactive it means that you wait for life to 'happen'. When an event occurs then you scurry and run wild like a chicken without a head trying to fix whatever has gone wrong with hopes that it will not happen again! Sooner than you think you are back at doing the same thing you hoped not to do, and it has become repetitive and frustrating! You don't bother to plan accordingly, you just wait and hope. On the other hand, to be proactive it means that you think about what you can do about situations by studying patterns.

Patterns are apparent when you are focused and determined. For example, in the past you may have driven your car until it was empty on gas just thinking you could go just a few more miles. Your car was always running out of gas often and you were always getting stuck on the road and having to call someone for help. You did this quite often and heard others repeatedly say "you need to get it together". You even thought, "There is nothing I can really do about it!" That was the reactive side of you! Now to make the switch to being proactive you may realize that there was a pattern involved with how you dealt with the situation and the outcome was always undesirable. Your speech now is "I will figure out a way to keep my car filled with gas by filling my tank on Sundays and put at least $20 in the tank every Thursday so I won't have to worry about running out of gas". You even take it a step further by budgeting $60 a week for gas and put the money aside just for that. You have a plan in place and not just one plan but maybe two or three. You anticipate what will occur, to an extent, and plan according to the outcome you desire. Now we know that we do not have total control over any outcome but as a proactive person, you seek the one that makes sense and put forth your best effort and put your trust in Allah because He has total control.

You see, being proactive means you take full responsibility for what happens to you. Simply put, YOU MAKE LIFE HAPPEN FOR YOU! You don't sit around finding excuses to stay stuck in situations and blame others for what happens or what goes wrong. You know that only you can truly plan and take action to change your circumstances. You are not choosing to complain, but willing to TAKE ACTION to make your situation better.

Time for A.C.T.I.O.N.

Grab a pen

Here are a few questions you may want to answer to realize if you are getting closer to shifting from a reactive life to one that is proactive. This is from the book "How to Get from Where You Are To Where You Want to Be: 25 Success Principles" *(Canfield, Jack. How to Get from Where You Are to Where You Want to Be: The 25 Principles of Success. HarperCollins Publishers, 2007.)*

1. How do I view the world around me?

2. Do I easily become annoyed with situations beyond my control?

3. Do I believe that you are responsible for what happens to others?

4. Do I think I am responsible for what happens to me?

5. Am I willing to give up worrying about things that I have no control over?

6. What can I do in my life that would bring about change?

7. When am I willing to start?

8. Who can I trust to help hold me accountable?

9. Am I willing to get help when needed?

10. Am I willing to "keep on keeping on" when I get stuck instead of giving up?

If you answered "no" to question(s) 2 and/or 3, answered "yes" to questions 1,4,5,9,and 10, and answered all other questions with ease then you might say that you are getting close to making a shift from being reactive to being proactive.

May Allah guide you to strive with ihsan(excellence) in all good things and may He guide you to take heed to His signs -Ameen!

Chapter 6 - Failing with grace - Knowing that Allah is in control

"The strong believer is better and more dear to Allah than the weak believer, and in each of them there is good. Be vigilant for what is to your benefit and seek the help of Allah and do not falter. But when you are stricken by some setback, do not say: 'If only I had done such and such,' rather say: 'It is the Decree of Allah and He does whatever He wills.' For verily the saying 'if (i.e. if only I had) begins the work of the Devil."

(Sahih Muslim 4/2052.)

We humans tend to feel worthless when we fail at something. Some of us just throw the towel in, giving up because of some small and temporary defeat. Just because we failed at something it does not mean that nothing else can be accomplished! The world's most successful people have failed at many things more times than average. They did not allow these small failures to change their minds about how great their ideas were. They strove hard despite the repetitive failing they endured. I know you know of many successful people in history that have failed but kept going when the going became tough. To name a few: The one thing that mattered most to them was their desire to win. Successful people don't start out great they become great. Becoming the person who you want to be is winning. Remaining to be the person you are is losing especially when you know you have the potential to be something better. You know the old saying "if at first you don't succeed Try, Try Again"? This is true but it is only how you perceive it. You may look at it as try once and if you fail try it again. Alright! That may work for some but let's try looking at it like this, "Try once and if you fail at it try twice as hard the next time". Continuing to use this method several times will only work for those who want success so bad in this life and the next that they will sacrifice everything they have.

Failing is an event it is not, by far, who you are when something does not go right or is not happening in your favor. Who do you blame for failure? You blame the event. You are still the wonderful person you are and remember the failure was only an event. It had to occur to give you measure and balance in what you were attempting to do. If you did not go towards what you believed would work then you would have been stuck in the "I wonder what would have happened" mode and then it may cause sadness. You may lose your awesomeness and creativity! You cannot afford that!

Fail with grace. I know that probably was the shortest sentence in history! Though that is such a short sentence it is very important. Failing with grace means to fail as much as you can, give thanks to The Creator for giving you the opportunity, loving yourself for it, that failing is a an event, and getting back up and pushing forward despite the challenges you may face. Don't get hung up on the number of times you fail at doing something, rather just realize that you found ways it would not work. Now this gives you time to go back and tweak your plan. It may take weeks, months, or (even) years before you actually see success but the key is to NEVER GIVE UP ON YOURSELF!! Too many others have died with great ideas to help shape the world but because they failed at one attempt they gave up the thought of being successful. Now they are gone and their ideas are too! This is sort of selfish. At least that is what it means to me. Here you have an idea that could help someone or others who may be struggling with something in the world and you decide to just GIVE UP! This is really unfair! I say you must GIVE IT UP! Get off of your ideas and work to manifest them. Someone out there needs what you have to offer! You have to fail at it more than a couple of times to make sure it's just right for them!

The next time you set out to do something, expect to fail after one or two attempts! If in fact, if you do fail, remember to GET UP, MAKE DUA (Pray to Allah), AND TRY TWICE AS HARD AS YOU DID THE LAST TIME! Fear has no place in the word fail, they are two separate words and their spelling and meanings are not the same. I know people like to use the phrase "fear of failing" but why not dare to be different and say I must fail at fearing! This is how you fail with grace. Nothing happens for no reason at all. Allah has a purpose and plan for all that comes to you and it is up to you to be patient, persevere and pray to him for guidance in all good things. He will not let you down! It is all in His decree. You have no control of the outcome of anything! Don't fall into the trap of saying "If I had done so and so" because it only invites the shaytaan to suggest that you are a failure and that nothing is possible or worthy of achieving! You may become depressed and unmotivated and you definitely don't want to be feeling like that! Take a deep breath, call on Allah immediately, and be grateful for the experience! Ask Him to guide you!

Say

"Qaddara llahi wa maa shaa fa'al"

It is the Decree of Allah and He does whatever He wills.

Time for A.C.T.I.O.N.

Set your timer for 15 minutes.

Grab a pen and paper (or write below)

Think about a time when you failed at something. Try to remember the details of the event and of the emotions you felt.

How did you react?_____

_____

_____

_____Did you give up or did you get back up and try again? Why? Or Why not?_____

_____

_____

_____

List your accomplishments (as many as you can).

_____
_____
_____
_____
_____
_____
_____
_____
_____
_____

How did each accomplishment make you feel?

_____
_____
_____
_____
_____
_____
_____
_____
_____
_____

Would you love to have these feelings again? If so, why did it mean so much?

_____
_____
_____
_____
_____
_____
_____

Write down at least 10 goals that you want to achieve over the next 10 years. (In all areas of your life)

Write down what it means to accomplish 3 of those goals and write:

I plan to fail fear in achieving this. Fear has no place, failing is only an event, I am awesome, Alhamdulilah, and I will achieve this, in shaa Allah! Allah has given me all that I need to make this happen. La Hawla Wa La Quwatta Ila billah- There is no might nor power except with Allah!

_____
_____
_____
_____
_____
_____
_____
_____

_____
_____
_____
_____
_____
_____
_____
_____
_____
_____
_____
_____

Now one thing that I am very big on is this thing called ACTION! These goals are nothing without action.

If you think you may need support in reaching your goals, please feel free to email me at **mmpermission2win@gmail.com** with "Goal Setting" in the subject line. In the message area please provide a number where I can reach you and a brief description of yourself and the goal or goals you want help in achieving.

May Allah help you to see beyond your failed attempts and lend more energy toward being resilient and successful in all good things-Ameen!

Chapter 7- Not the "Asiyyah of all trades"

God does not burden any human being with more than he is well able to bear. *(The Noble Quran 2: 286)*

The motivated Muslimah realizes that she does not have to know how and do everything, and that it is almost impossible to. By nature being the "Asiyyah of All Trades", does not work to your advantage when running a business and maintaining family life. Somebody or something that is very important, stands the chance of being totally neglected when we attempt to.

So, how does she deal with this dying need to do everything? She values her time and prioritizes tasks in a manner that allows her to perform tasks that she can perform because she possesses the knowledge and skill to do so. She also leverages tasks that she is not able to do because of her lack of knowledge or skills. She develops a team of individuals that she can rely on to perform tasks that she is unable to perform. Maybe she has no time to send out invoices, or sort, check and send email, or post to social media. She needs to outsource these tasks so that she can spend quality time with her family and on what she does best. Most importantly she must take a break from all this mayhem to remember her own importance

I had to learn this the hard way actually! When I began building my website for my organization, Herspiring Bizness, I just thought "what skills do you really need to build a simple website?" Little did I know that I would stick to my laptop for the next two weeks straight, trying to create this "SIMPLE" website. Oh My! The only thing simple about the whole ordeal was the words that read "As Easy As 123"! I learned that I could have saved so much time and could have used that time with being productive in tasks that I knew how to perform like marketing to prospects, coaching, writing articles for my blog and Facebook business page, ordering business cards and promotional items, writing for this book that you are reading developing my business plan etc... I know it seems like its "NO BIG DEAL" right? The problem here is that all other tasks were being neglected! I was glued to my laptop for at least 8 hours or more a day! My children had gotten so used to me sitting on the living room sofa in the same spot day after day and started to make comments like "Ummi why don't you just pay somebody who knows how to do it", "can we please go outside because we have been waiting all day", "Ummi we are hungry can you please fix dinner or tell us what we could fix?", etc.. They made sure that I knew I was neglecting them if nothing else!

Time for A.C.T.I.O.N.- Acquiring Confidence To Initiate Opportunity Now

Ok, now that you realize you have been just doing way too much and some things and people are being neglected because of it, what will you do about it?

Time for A.C.T.I.O.N.

Grab a pen

Set your timer for 15 minutes or not more than 20, if necessary.

Jot down a list of all tasks to be performed on a daily basis in your business

Place a check next to those tasks that you know you could do without much struggle and that you possess the knowledge and skills to perform. Be Honest!

Place an X next to those tasks that you have been performing but have struggled with even though you completed them. Be Honest!

Count the number of checks and X's separately. If the number of tasks with an X next to them outnumber the tasks with a check next to them then you have got some leveraging to do my dear sister!

Pick at least three of those tasks which you placed an X next to. I hope you realize by now that they will need OTHER people's expertise, time, knowledge assigned to them. What say you? Start thinking of friends, ex-coworkers, school mates, or even professionals that you can afford to pay. I recommend that firs, you ask from those who just want to help you in your mission and are not assigning a dollar amount to the tasks they perform, then the ones who want to be compensated but it is within your budget, make sure that they are people who don't have a problem with being held accountable to what they say they will do. Make a chart of tasks and who will perform them and when they should have each task completed. Mark each task as it is completed. Try this method for at least 3 weeks and see if things start looking good.

Now as you do all of this, remember those things and people you were neglecting and put forth the necessary effort to give them your attention. It is my hope that you will become more at ease and that things will be running much smoother than they were before.

May Allah grant you ease in all of your difficulties and may He grant you success in all your endeavors-Ameen!

Chapter 8- Saying "NO" with humble confidence

The Prophet Muhammad (saw) said: "Be kind, for whenever kindness becomes part of something, it beautifies it. Whenever it is taken from something, it leaves it tarnished". *(Imam Bukhari's Book of Muslim Manners.)*

You know that feeling you get when you have to turn down someone's request? Well for those of us who know the feeling it is very uncomfortable and if we can avoid it, we most certainly will. If you're a "people pleaser", like I was for a very long time, it is hard for you especially because you don't want to lose your relationships be it business, family, or personal ones. You want to be liked so you will give in to every request until you practically pass out from being overwhelmed. Sometimes the friends you had before you started changing old habits into new and more effective ones, like this one, decide that they no longer want to be your friend because they feel hurt. You have to do your best to explain to them that you want to be there for them as much as you can, however, right now you are not able to do so. Sometimes giving a small gift or sending them a nice card letting them know you still care about them can go along way and buffer that NO word! Granted, some people you have to say no to because they want to be nosy enough about what you are involved with so that they can sabotage your efforts and make you feel like what you are doing is just useless.

Well what if I could share with you some tips on how to make a habit of saying no with confidence? Would you be willing to take notes? If so, go grab a pen and let's begin!

Time for A.C.T.I.O.N.

The next time you want to turn down a request try these alternatives to just saying "NO":

1. Try saying I am not able to help you with that right now, its because I am really busy

2. Do you need help with that right away or can you give me a specific date

3. As soon as I am finished with what I am doing I will give you a call, in shaa Allah

4. Can you give me a moment to see if I can fit this into my schedule?

5. Thank you for that awesome idea, however, I am not interested at this time! Check back with me in a few days, weeks, months, because things sure do change often!

These are only a few of the ways you could say no without actually saying no in the real sense!

Now I want you to explore your own journey of saying no and feeling confident about it!

List the reasons why you think you have a hard time saying no

_____
_____
_____
_____
_____
_____
_____
_____
_____

_____

Next list the people you absolutely have a hard time saying no to.

_____
_____
_____
_____
_____
_____
_____
_____

_____
_____

Order this list from least difficulty to most difficulty

_____
_____
_____
_____
_____
_____
_____
_____
_____

_____

Think of the last time you had to say no to any of these people. What was their reaction? What was your
reaction?_____
_____
_____
_____
_____
_____
_____
_____
_____

Write down some possible situations in which you would have to turn down an opportunity? (Speaking engagement, workshop, invite to an event etc...) _____

_____
_____
_____
_____
_____
_____
_____

I know that you are probably thinking that you have to grab on and hold every opportunity that comes your way because you're an entrepreneur but it does not have to be that way. It is natural to fear that if you turn down opportunity, you may lose money. And not just lose some money, in fact it may be that the money you lose was very much needed. Whoa! I know that this sounds crazy but it may do you more harm than good if you did not investigate the opportunity for the dramatic loss it could incur in the long run, instead of the immediate gratification it serves NOW!!! This does not mean that you should start thinking negative thoughts about every opportunity scaring yourself into more disbelief about the good that it could bring you or your business but the lesson here is to DO YOUR HOMEWORK before saying yes! It may save you a lot of trouble in the long run!

Okay for you self- saboteurs, I know you are probably saying "this is why I just look at the worst that could happen first and then decide that I won't even bother"! The idea here is not to analyze the heck out of the opportunity until you become 'paralyzed'. Paralysis of analysis is common to you self-saboteurs! It masks your fear of failure or success. You end up spending way too much time on why the opportunity is not good for you, instead of weighing the good and the bad of the opportunity proportionately. Think of it this way. If something does not turn out the way you want it only means that way did not work or that opportunity was not IT!!! It does not mean you are a failure! The event failed but you are still a great person. Awesomeness is in you!

Again, realize that when you are saying no to something or someone you are saying YES to someone else or something else. You are saying yes to what is more important, I hope! I know that as an entrepreneur saying no could mean that you just want to go and hide from the chaos that may be happening in your biz and that is understandable but let's get into those no's that keep you moving despite your emotion about it.

The next time you have to decide on saying no to something, write it down in a journal.

Be honest about how hard it was to say no and how it made you feel your fears. Also record the outcome or result of your decision on the situation. What did you say yes to and how beneficial was it to say no instead of yes? Since this book is all about habits I suggest you write your NO's in this journal for the next 2 1/2 months to record your NO's. Look at the previous entries before placing a new one each time to reflect on it and embrace the outcome whether it was favorable or not. Say "I am saying No because even if I said yes NO was still an option. If you were told that you had no option but to say yes you would automatically want to find a way that you could say no; it's just our nature. We were born with the free will of choice so when we the threat of having no choice is upon us we will become uncomfortable and want to challenge it. May Allah keep you humble- Ameen!

Chapter 9- She consistently seeks to get out of her own way when embarking on her goal.

'O Allah, it is your mercy that I hope for, so do not leave me in charge of my affairs even for a blink of an eye and rectify for me all of my affairs. None has the right to be worshipped except you.'

(http://ahadith.co.uk/hisnulmuslim-dua-35 :The Fortress of a Muslim)

Getting out of your own way involves replacing negative emotional habits with positive ones. Negative emotional habits are thoughts that you perceive about yourself. You convince yourself that these thoughts are true without any proof. It's just that simple! You use it as a way to cut off your opportunities both intentionally and unintentionally. When you become fearful of achieving your goals this is a sure way to not work towards achieving at all. Maybe if you thought better about yourself you could at least find ways to become motivated.

The highly productive and striving Muslimah works often to remove negative emotional habits. She understands that they just stand in the way of her achieving success. She knows that it is the shaytaan the devil who is suggesting that she short change herself and give up. She will feel pain along the journey just like anyone else but she chooses to empower herself to win!

The truth about getting stuck is that you are the one making yourself stuck. You fail once and just give up, thinking it was never meant to be. This is self- defeat. This negative emotional roller coaster of feeling guilty, inferior, fear, inadequate, abandoned, etc... You are simply stuck in your emotions! It's like you won't allow yourself to feel it and let it motivate you to shift to better emotions. It feels good to have an excuse why you won't persevere and it sounds good to others around you. You know there is a possibility that others will pass you the "pity couch" and let you sulk in your emotions. You know exactly what I am talking about! Yes! Pity party time! The sad part about this is that you waste good time and energy that could have been used towards achieving your goals.

Time for A.C.T.I.O.N.

Let's talk about some of the more common negative emotions that many people possess. If one of these listed below resonates with you I want you to stop and feel the emotion, take notice of why you feel this way, and ask yourself the following questions;

Do I like this feeling? What is the reason for this feeling? What price am I paying for sticking to this emotion? Is there any benefit for feeling like this? How willing am I to trade this feeling or shift it for a more positive one? What will I do to make this shift? When will I start? Who can I count on to check up on my progress?

Grab a pen and paper or use the space below.

Set your timer for 20 minutes.

Make dua for relief of anxiety and stress.

Here is list a of a few common negative emotions;

Insulted

Let down

Irritated

Abandoned

Abused

Defeated

Violated

Guilt Tripped

Inadequate

Doubtful

Humiliated

Intimidated

For a more comprehensive list of negative emotions go to http://negativeemotionslist.com/

How about joining us at Herspiring Bizness for a live webinar on identifying negative emotional habits, and tips on how to shift to positive and motivating ones?

Great! I thought you would never ask! Send us an email to mmpermission2win@gmail.com with "Making Shifts" in the subject area. My executive assistant will be more than happy to follow up with you to further explain the details on how to join the webinar.

To clear your subconscious you would have to give it new information. Well how do you take out the old information? Good question! You cannot just take it out but you can replace it with new information that suggests overcoming your fears, removing self- limiting beliefs, and building self-confidence and self-esteem. We most also remember that the shaytaan is always at work. He works the 12 to 12 shift so there is really know way of totally avoiding him. You have got to have a plan of action to avert him whenever he suggests and attempts to validate your fears

First of all stop telling yourself you are not capable of doing something when you have not even tried. Quitting can only occur after you have tried something so you don't even have that as an option unless you act! The negative thoughts you have about your capabilities will harbor in your subconscious and validate your fear.

May Allah guide you to be confident in your abilities to achieve success-Ameen!

Chapter 10-She trains her subconscious mind

"Whether you hide your word or publish it. He certainly has full knowledge of the secrets of all hearts. He is the One that understands the finest mysteries and is well-acquainted with them." *(The Noble Quran 67:13-14)*

Your subconscious mind is your partner in success. It is not just a figment of your imagination, as we were told when we were little girls. It actually works hand in hand with our conscious minds. One of the functions of the subconscious mind is that it attracts conditions and circumstances to us according to the predominant pattern of thinking that it holds. It will always act upon what it stores as a result of your thoughts.

Now I know you have probably heard of what a vision board is, right? There was a big phenomenon after the release of the movie "The Secret". Everyone was tapping into their visions because they somehow thought that if they believed in the law of attraction, it could bring them things that they desired. I am not knowledgeable about the Laws of Physics nor am I any Scholar but I know that the subconscious mind is something magnificent that Allah created us with and has functions that many people know little or nothing about.

Thoughts repeated frequently will implant in the subconscious mind, however, this part of the mind does not distinguish the reality from fantasy. This is the reason why visualization has such a powerful effect on us. When you watch television it happens often. These images get implanted and if done often, they may become part of your belief system and dictate your behavior. No wonder some scholars say that television is from the shaytaan. Be aware of this tool of shaytaan to suggest to you what is wrong is fair seeming. Be moderate and stay on point!

Our conscious minds need to be fed well because it holds the key to our subconscious mind. I cannot say it enough! It must only accept thoughts that will be beneficial to our lives in dunya and prepare us for the Akhirah(Hereafter). It is believed that the self-affirmations fed to the subconscious mind are best done in an already achieved mode. It is also important to be honest with yourself. Some personal development gurus suggest shouting incantations. I suggest you use affirmations to empower yourself and build your self-esteem and confidence to achieve your goals but there is something that needs to be explained here, especially for the Muslimah. These incantations are not the same as affirmations because they are literally spells and we don't want to trap ourselves into repeating the speech of those who carry them. It's no coincidence that one famous personal development guru got people to walk across hot coals! The truth is that once a person is convinced that they can do anything whether they convince themselves or someone else convinces them, it seems almost impossible for them not to achieve it or at least take action. The endorphins in the brain release giving this person the burning feeling that they can and that is fine if what they shout is not in conflict with their belief system. Incantations are just not a part of the belief system of a Muslim. It would be better for us to recite the Quran and make dua(prayer). This is the incantation that this famous personal development guru shouted out every day once he made a decision to become a millionaire within a year's time, "God's wealth is circulating in my life. His wealth flows to me in avalanches of abundance. All my needs, desires and goals are met instantaneously. For, I am one with God, and God is everything."

What is wrong with this? Why won't it work for you?

Well for one, he has convinced himself that he is one with Allah and you know, very well, that is not possible. Allah says in Quran:

"-Say: He is Allah, The One and Only! Allah, The Eternal, Absolute; He begetteth not nor is He begotten. And there is none equal to Him" *(The Noble Quran;Surah Al- Ihklas)* May Allah guide this man to the truth-Ameen!

May Allah forgive me for anything that I have written in error-Ameen!

When a person believes something about themselves whether it be negative or positive they are giving their subconscious minds cues to dictate their behavior. If they believe that they are a horrible writer they will never finish the book they always wanted to write because they have defeated themselves internally. Their subconscious now suggests that there is no use in taking action to write that book and most likely they won't. The result of this is low self- esteem and self -worth. This thought will now dictate how they behave because it is what the subconscious has been given as a cue to act on.

If you think about it, this is how imperialized lands ruled over the people. They convinced their subjects to believe they were inferior and worth nothing. Now you know it is way too easy to conquer someone who believes they are already conquered than to try and fight someone who knows there self-worth, right? This is just the same about someone telling you that you are worthy and good at some particular trade or skill. You can even say this to yourself in the mirror. It is what is perceived that holds the key to how one will behave. It also affects reality, but it does not change it. Reality is reality as Allah has created it. We as Muslims must always seek to be at peace with the reality that exists in our lives. Only Allah can truly change the reality.

If you have no money, it is a reality but if you shift your thoughts about your Lack of money to one that suggests money is not what you lack but it is the belief in the opportunities that exist in order for you to attain your provision. Put your trust in Allah and ask that He (Allah) guide you to those opportunities and may He purify your intentions- Ameen!

You must train your conscious mind to think that Money is only the means it is not the end. Allah will open more doors of opportunity for you. Allah is your provision, so believe in Him and strengthen your relationship with Him and it will bring you the best in prosperity and much needed hope in adversity!

So to wrap this all up, know that positive affirmations are used to encourage self- esteem and motivate one to strive harder and set the bar high for themselves instead of settling and imprisoning themselves with internal oppression.

You don't have to lie to yourself because it will never work for you. Many of us find it hard to lie so our subconscious cannot accept what we truly don't believe. Say "I believe that I am good at_____ because even though I have failed at it, I am willing to do whatever I can to make it happen, bi'ithnillah(with Allah's permission)! I really want_____ so I will keep striving until I make it no matter how tough it gets or how long it takes me, in shaa Allah!

Remember Hadith Qudsi, when the Prophet Muhammad(sallalahu alayhi wa salam) said, "The Most High said, I am as my servant thinks I am. I am with him when he mentions Me. If he mentions Me to himself, I mention him to myself, and if he mentions Me in assembly, I mention him in an assembly greater than it. If he draws near to Me a hand's length I draw near to him an arm's length. And if he comes to Me walking, I go to him at speed".

Ibn Hajar(RA) said, on this hadith, that it means Allah is saying "I am able to do whatever he expects I will do"*(Fath Al Bari)*

You want success? Have hope and long for relief if you truly believe in The One Who is The Source of Relief- Al Basit. Be aware of what you plant in your subconscious mind because remember it will give you cues to act on and you want those cues to be positive and suggesting righteousness in actions. The deeper your connection is with Allah the better off your conscious and subconscious mind will be.

Time for A.C.T.I.O.N.

Set your timer for 20 minutes

Grab a pen and answer the questions below

1-What am I dissatisfied about? (i.e. no time to spend with family, working too much, I hate my job, I am too fat, I am too skinny etc...)

List at most, 7 things. Then circle 3 that you want to focus on._____

_____
_____
_____
_____

_____
_____

2-What is it costing me to remain dissatisfied?(ie. guilt, sadness, regret etc...)Only in regards to the three you circled above._____
_____
_____
_____
_____
_____
_____

3-What is the reality of my current situation? (in those three areas)_____
_____
_____
_____
_____
_____

4-Can I accept the reality? _____ If no, STOP HERE!! You have to be willing to accept reality because it allows you to deal with your dissatisfaction in a more sincere way. Why lie to yourself. Your subconscious won't accept it because your deeper feelings about it exist, and that it's the reality. Telling yourself the truth and accepting it is the first step in bringing about change. You don't need to beat yourself up about it or sulk but just realize that what IS and now you will take advantage of the opportunity to do something!

5-What do I want to happen instead of what is happening? In other words, what do I want to shift? (Without saying "this is my goal")_____
_____
_____
_____
_____
_____

6-Is it possible? _____ (If it is not, STOP HERE!) If you don't see the possibility then you won't want it bad enough to MAKE IT HAPPEN!) JUST GIVE UP!!! NO ONE CAN HELP YOU TO WANT SOMETHING BAD ENOUGH TO GET IT BUT YOU!!!Your motivation comes from within in. Yeah! Sure! Words that you hear or read are motivating and can get you moving but when you realize the motivation inside of you it's an indescribable feeling! You become almost unstoppable and highly productive in your thoughts and actions towards achieving your goals! Your striving is sincere and authentic and very hard to discourage!!!!

7-What do I need to do in order to make this shift? What is my plan of action? Think in stages. What will I do today, then tomorrow or next week, next month etc... Even if it is a small task, as long as it falls in line with the bigger picture it is worth it. You don't have to over -do it!_____

_____
_____
_____
_____
_____
_____
_____
_____
_____

8-What exactly am I willing to do to make this shift? Be Honest! You don't have to start being superwoman just be you! You know what are willing to do vs. what you think you should do or what others think you should do._____

_____
_____

9-Why do I want to make this shift?(Your WHY needs to be BIG enough in order to MOTIVATE you to ACT and remain PRODUCTIVE- Your why needs to make you CRY)_____
_____
_____
_____
_____

10-Who do I need to become in order to achieve this?_____
_____
_____
_____
_____

11-What obstacles do I think will be in the way?_____
_____
_____
_____
_____

12-Should I meet any one of these obstacles/setbacks while making the shift what is my plan for resilience? Note to self..."I know that my setback is only a temporary layoff giving me the energy I need for a strong COMEBACK! I must turn to Allah, subhannah wa ta'ala, and ask for which way I should go so that I am in line with what His plan is for me and not get hung up on my plan for me. His plan is always the BEST because He is in TOTAL CONTROL and THAT'S IT THAT'S ALL"!!!_____

_____
_____
_____
_____

13-When will I begin taking ACTION? Start today! Motivation is probably steaming in your blood right now, so keep it hot! Don't do all of this hard work at planning and then put off the execution of it! You know the saying "why put off until tomorrow what you could do today"~author unknown_ - Also Also think "What is one small step I can take to today to get me closer to my goal?_____

_____
_____
_____
_____
_____

14- What do I expect to happen, immediately, once I begin making this shift?_____
_____
_____
_____
_____

15- Who can I rely on for support as I work towards making this shift? First and foremost you reliance should be on Allah, subhannah wa ta'ala! Don't just list your close friends! You want those people who are going to make you feel uncomfortable and not feel bad about it because they want to see you win! They are going to let you know when you are slipping! You also do not want any negative people filling your head with all of their thoughts about how impossible it is to achieve what you are trying to achieve. Later for them! Keep them as friends of course, but they are not the kind of support you need in this situation. You're on a mission beloved!

_____
_____

_____
_____
_____
_____

16-How will I hold myself accountable?_____

_____
_____
_____
_____
_____

17-How will I know that I have met success?(what does it look like?)_____

_____
_____
_____
_____
_____

—

18-How will I celebrate my success? Don't get shy now! You deserve to celebrate your successes no matter how big or small they are! Say Alhamdulilah! Allahu Akbar, SubhannAllah as soon as you meet success and treat yourself to

something or some place nice!_____
_____
_____
_____
_____
_____
_____
_____
_____

Now your subconscious is ready for that statement you will make almost every day to keep you in the productive and striving mode you need to be in order to make your shift!

What will you say to your beautiful subconscious? _(here is what I say...I know that I am not comfortable with my weight but I am willing to do what is necessary to make a shift in how I treat my beautiful body given to me by Allah every day that I live so that I can feel better about myself. In shaa Allah I will eat what is good for me and exercise daily._____
_____
_____
_____
_____
_____

May Allah increase you in knowledge of things that would benefit you and the ability to apply it- Ameen!

Chapter 11-Taking 100% Responsibility for your life-

Allah will not change the condition of a people until they change the condition in their hearts

In April of 2013 I was given a book that forced me to start removing my fears about changing my circumstances for the better. The name of the book was called "Who Moved My Cheese *(Spencer Johnson. Who Moved My Cheese?. Penguin Group (USA)* At first I admit I was not wowed by it but as I continued to read it became difficult to put the book down! It was not long after I read this book when I realized that everyone fit in at some sort level or stage of change.

Some people are Hemmers -not at all realizing that change will eventually have to happen in order to grow or Haws- Though it does feel scary moving through change, it will become easier to accept once you begin to realize that your cheese has MOVED and that it is time to find NEW CHEESE despite your fears and EMBRACE the ADVENTURE while picking up little pieces of ASSURITY along the way or Sniffers-You are always on the lookout for OPPORTUNITIES to change or better yet you smell when a change is coming on before it is actually presented to you so you stand READY or Scurries- You don't waste time moving on to find NEW Cheese because you know that the old cheese is definitely GONE and ITS TIME to MOVE on in full force despite your obstacles and you are willing to learn and discover what is behind those walls that you kept avoiding for so long ,because you feared that you may get lost, hoping to discover New Cheese of all kinds! What I understood in total was that change is inevitable and that even when something is going good and it has lasted for a very long time; it too is subjected to change. On the flip side, when something is not going so well and you don't seek to move on and change the circumstance for fear of loss or whatever is your fear, you lose hope of it ever changing and stay in the familiar to avoid that fear. Trust in Allah and know that he does not desire difficulty and that He can make the difficult easy! I speak to my own self first because my eyes are the first to see this message before yours and my mouth is closer to my two ears than it is to yours. We must prepare ourselves to move with the cheese whatever it is (marriage, business, health etc.) and walk through our fears to get what we truly desire in this life and in the next. El Hajj Malik Shabazz said not only "By Any Means Necessary" but he also said "It's a pity that if opportunity were to present itself we would not even be ready". Oh! I forgot to mention that I was a Haw for a very long time but I had too many Hems around me. You would not truly understand unless you read the book for yourself.

The reason I began this section with change is because in order to take full responsibility of your precious life you must realize where you are in life, either accept it and be settled or make an effort to shift to a more desired lifestyle. When I was reading, Who Moved My Cheese, I had to be honest with what was going on in my life. Everything was definitely not peachy! I had a lot to be thankful for and I also had a lot that I was regretful for. Being regretful weighed heavier than being thankful. I knew I wanted to make a clean shift to a more positive and healthier life but I needed to deal with my issues of regret. I had to have a purpose in order to begin moving forward, and my purpose started to become clear. My purpose for wanting to change my circumstances was no big secret anymore. I wanted life before death and not a dead life before death. I mean what was the purpose of living dead? Anyone who decides that, has surely forgotten about the most important reason for living. The Creator created us for one purpose and that is to worship Him and living is not an option if you are alive and breathing. This sounds so smoothly put but can very difficult to digest if you have been living dead for so long and have allowed your bad experiences to decide whether you should exist or not. You have been choosing to react to your past in ways that block your path of possibilities. You have been choosing to allow your pain to dictate your movements and passing over opportunities to change your life for the better. You believe that your past has shaped who you are and it has become useless to reach for the stars and become different. I know all too well how it feels to be like this and the pain you carry is actually what keeps you feeling sorry for yourself because you believe that the only one crying for you is you! You don't believe that anyone else can feel your pain and so you push away just about anyone who looks like they want to help you. You close every door of possibility to relieve your pain because you have become so comfortable with holding it within. Holding it within gives you a sense of power over whoever or whatever hurt you. Forgiveness is really not even an option and you lie to yourself saying you forgive and have moved on in front of others who suggest it to keep them from encouraging you to forgive so that you could hold on to your power or control longer. This is known as resentment and it is what you eat, sleep, breath, laugh and cry almost every day of your life and what stands as your body guard to block any more threats of pain. You judge yourself before giving the opportunity to others to get to know you. This is because you fear deeply that they will cause you to let your guard down and let go of your pain and resentment and that would just kill you to do that! You have not even perceived life without this and so any threat to remove it seems scary. You wear a fake smile to hide your pain and you don't build on relationships because you just don't trust people. Everyone is suspect! Anything that appears to be a suggestion to let go of pain and the past and to forgive, heal, and move forward is just too difficult for you. Shutting out the world around you makes you feel comfortable and in control of your life. You will only truly love people who allow you to remain like this because they don't challenge you to become uncomfortable with your circumstance. Any major change in your life will require some sort of challenge.

The real challenge is when you face your life head on and stop pointing the finger at everyone else for what has happened in your life up until now. You have got to remove the blame and upgrade your life. You have got to realize that your time is now and you are going to have to start changing your responses to events that happen in your life as well as make decisions based upon how you want to live your life. You cannot just sit there and wait for life to just happen! That is what got you to the point you are at now! You have to live your life on purpose. You have to make it happen. I know you may not want move completely out of the space of pain because it gives you an excuse on your rainy days but rainy days don't have to be bad days, in fact rainy days for a Muslim are blessed days and great days to seek from Allah. It's time you forgive yourself and anyone who has hurt you and caused you to be hurt. Your heart and mind need a break from all that it's been enduring. How dare you weigh them down with your burden for as long as you did? The heart is made to love and the mind is made to learn. What you learn you will eventually love if it is what you desire. I encourage you to learn about Allah, your worth and give your heart the room to love you! You cannot give love if you cannot love you. All the happiness you are searching for emanates from you. There is no outside force that will break the good news of happiness to you. You also have to be ready! Be ready to show up in your life because it's going to take work! An employee who wants pay at the end of a hard week of work has to show up to work. You already have what you need because that is how we were created. Allah did not create the Earth without vegetation and all that you need. Do yourself a favor and evict yourself from that ol' rundown apartment of your life that you have spent years trying to patch up. You never really fixed anything and now nothing is worth fixing. You're going to have to tear it down to the ground and rebuild a new residence! Your foundation needs to consist of strength, courage, trust, *eeman(faith)*, confidence, discipline, and resilience. You can add more pillars or walls that are reflective of your new life as you level up. Whether you are divorced, recovering from drug addiction or alcoholism, homeless, just released from prison, in prison, a victim of domestic abuse(childhood/adult) etc.. You have to rise above your circumstances and excuses so that you can truly shine your light! You are the reason why you are going through what you go through today. The event happened but your reaction to it was your decision. You made the decision to allow others to have power over you by holding on to the hurt instead of forgiving. You made the choice to drink or to use just one more time because it felt good to you. You run from your problems and never dealt with them. You chose to not forgive who hurt you. You even chose not to forgive yourself. You chose to impulsively blow money and now you're broke. You chose to eat unhealthy, knowing how dangerous it is for your health. You chose not to exercise and now it's too late. You chose not to guard your salat (prayer) , waiting for the perfect time and now you are experiencing hard trials and calling everyone but Allah when He commanded that you seek from Him. You chose to stay in that toxic abusive relationship for as long as you did for fear of losing someone who did not even love you anyway. You chose to stay at your dead end job even though the pay sucked. You chose to not live your passion and get paid for it. You chose to say no to opportunity after opportunity to make your life happen for fear of failing. You chose! You Chose You Chose! Now it's time to choose again! This time you have to be aware of what you chose so that you begin living the life you desire and stop making choices based on your bad emotional habits. You have what it takes you just have to deliver!

I remember everything, like it was yesterday, when I decided to stop blaming others for what has happened and what was happening in my life. I knew that previously throughout a decade and half of my life I was saying that my past experience of rape at the age of 10 to 12 was something of the past and that I had forgiven the guy that did it to me. The truth was that I had never really forgave him. I blamed him for robbing me of my childhood. I was only able to do some things that normal teenagers did because of my mother's determination to keep me as normal as possible but I believe she knew I felt different. I wanted to be normal and thought that going to parties and school dances were a part of that. I went but that was not to feel normal that was the way I felt I could keep others from judging me. I mean I never wanted anyone to know that the reason I could not hang out was because I had a baby! I would have been talked about by everyone at school and my reputation of being cool with everybody would have just been ruined. I did not want to risk that at all! I lived a life of destruction since the day I gave birth to my eldest son just two months short of my 13 birthday. My destruction was internal and I made sure that no one knew what was really happening to me on the inside. I feared that I would be judged and just tortured. What place would a girl at 13 feel like she could fit in after such a tragic experience? My friends would not understand any of this! I believed that the less they knew about what had happened to me the better my life would be. I hid the birth of my child for the next 20 years of my life! Only a few of the children I grew up with knew my secret. I felt ashamed of my body and I believed that I was damaged goods not worth marriage to a real man who would take care of me and treat me like a Queen. Mr. X was the one responsible for me hating older men since he sought to show me what a boy would do on a date if I was not strong enough to push him off of me. Basically he scared the hell out of me and I never trusted him again. He is who I blamed for my panic attacks whenever I would see old men who take interest in younger girls and little girls close with their dads or uncles or any male for that matter. He told my sister and me that we could date once we were 15 years old which was totally against Islam. My mother was not aware of this! We did not tell her either! So that meant that any boy, my age, who would even act as if he took interest in me I would be suckered and taken advantage of. What a horrible life for a teenage girl! I gave into a lot of peer pressure short of drugs and alcohol because I just wanted to fit in. I could not bear the thought of even getting high or drunk since I had a family member who scared the life out of me with their drug habit and another family member who would drink his head off and throw things at my mother, breaking glass. The screams from the women in my family when they would find drug paraphernalia in my grandmother's basement just pierced my little heart making me frightened and I swore every time I heard it that I would never touch drugs. If they only knew what their screams did to me! As for Mr. X, whenever he would get drunk he would fight Mrs. X and break glass all over the place. It was devastating to say the least. I made a vow to never touch alcohol because of this horrifying experience. These two family members eventually stopped their habits but it took quite a toll on me and I never really had too much respect for either one of them after that. I knew that life had to be better than what I was seeing because as we would visit the masjid. I saw beautiful families where the mother and father and children just looked like they were happy. I just wanted a family like they had. I just knew my dream would come true someday.

Let me say that it had been about 25 years of blaming myself and others for how unhappy my life was. I blamed my mother for not protecting me from sexual abuse. I blamed my father for not being there to help me, I blamed, my family for not really understanding my internal pain, I blamed my sister for calling me such disgusting names the day she found out I was pregnant, I blamed my brother for not telling my mom when he would see on occasion what was happening to me but was threatened not to tell, I blamed myself for not fighting this abuse, I blamed myself for not telling someone it was happening to me. I blamed myself for the fondling done to me by Mr. X. I blamed him for my dislike of older men. I blamed my ex-husband for not being there for me the way I wanted him to be even though I never really showed him. I blamed my ex-husband for not being the man I needed him to be though I knew that he was too young to understand. I blamed myself for wanting to be normal. I blamed myself for hiding such a beautiful child for fear of how others would judge me. I blamed myself for having more children after I vowed to never have anymore because the memory of giving birth age at 12 was too tragic for me. I am the one who thought of taking my life at age 13 because the pain was too deep. I blamed myself for going away to college and leaving my son. I blamed myself for not having standards and just accepted any story from any random guy who only wanted to use me. I blamed myself for allowing men to take advantage of me because I was too afraid to stand up for myself. I blamed myself for being physically abused by a man. I blamed myself for thinking marriage would heal my deep scars of abuse and depression. I blamed myself for the events that took place in my unhappy marriage. I blamed myself for putting my trust in my ex-husband over and over. I blame myself for putting my kids through all that they went through. I blame myself for marrying a man who I did not know would not be able to father my son with love. I blame myself for what my ex-husband did to him. I blamed myself for not standing up for him more than I did. I blamed myself for how the state took my brother away. I blamed myself for not standing up for myself in my last marriage. I blamed myself for how my son has chosen to look for love in all the wrong places and getting himself into so much trouble. I chose to give up on my life but the bottom line to all of this is that I was the one who chose those thoughts, feelings, and behaviors, however, blaming myself and others would do me no good. I had gotten myself to where I was because of I never took full responsibility for what was happening in my life! It was time I had realized that in order to get from where I was to where I wanted to be in life I had to give up blaming and start forgiving. The day I finally asked my ex-husband for a divorce after 15 years of unhappiness was the day I realized that I was going to have to appreciate the person Allah created me to be and all He had given to me. It felt like the hardest day of my life but has proven to be an opportunity full of blessings! He had given me the opportunity to start again and to live again and I have decided to make my life happen. I not only chose to divorce my ex-husband but I chose to divorce the years of playing the blame game and allowing unhappiness to fill my life. I also chose to forgive myself and others, to seek Allah's forgiveness for myself and others, to be happy, to feel confident, to know my self-worth, and to put my love and trust in Allah first and foremost.

Time for A.C.T.I.O.N. (Read all the way through before taking action)

You will repeat this exercise once a day for the next 21 days.

Look for a quiet spot.

Relax your body (let the shoulders fall, wiggle your fingers, wiggle your toes)

Begin making dua to Allah to put you at ease and relieve you of distress and worry

(dua for anxiety or any dua seeking relief)

Place your hand on your chest over the spot where your heart resides

Begin breathing in through your nose and out of your mouth slowly (3 or 4 times).

Set your timer for at least 15 minutes but no more than 20

Day 1- Begin to slowly think about who you blame for the unhappiness in your life and why you blame them. If you blame yourself this counts too!

Day 2- Begin to slowly think about who you are willing to forgive. If it happens to be yourself, this counts too! Forgiveness is really hard if you have been holding on to resentment for some time. You will need time to actually forgive so don't worry yourself with that part right beloved! Read the chapter on forgiveness for deeper discovery.

Day 3- Begin to slowly think about where you are in life and where you would like to be!

Day 4- Begin to slowly think about why you want to be where you want to be and what will it do for you?

When the timer is up, grab your pen and begin writing below. Write all that took place in your meditation each day. Don't hold back anything! I know you will begin to feel either angry, disappointed, guilty, betrayed, ashamed, hurt etc… but eventually you will begin to feel relieved, empowered, anxious etc.... Don't Give Up!!! It's a part of the process. Do this for about 20 min. Stay focused. There is page here for the first three days to get you started but I suggest you purchase a journal to do this exercise.

Day1_____
_____
_____
_____

Day2_____

Day3_____

May Allah grant you relief from all that you have been holding within your heart and give you better than it-Ameen!

I am very interested in hearing about your discovery! I want you to move forward despite the negative feelings you have about your past experiences. Send me an email to mmpermission2win@gmail.com with "Motivated Muslimah" in the subject line.

Chapter 12-Treating the Body as an Amanah (trust from Allah)

"When the heart and the mind are in sync the limbs have no choice but to obey its commands, start your journey towards change within your heart and mind and put your trust in Allah"~Ukhtee Walida

As Muslimahs we have a duty to take care of the many trusts that Allah has given to us. The word for trust in Arabic is amanah. It is seen several times throughout the Quran to remind the believer of their duty to take care of what Allah has entrusted them with by following specific instructions. We must utilize these trusts as a means to earn Allah's mercy and in preparation for The Day when all souls will return to Him. This trust was given to us when the heavens and the mountains refused it. Proof of this is in *(The Noble Quran;Surah Al Ahzab :72)*

Allah says

"Surely we offered the trust to the heavens and the earth and the mountains, but they refused to undertake it and feared from it, but man undertook it; surely he is unjust, ignorant"

The word amana comes from the root word Alif Meem, Noon *(Wehr,Hans. A Dictionary of Modern Written Arabic: (Arabic-English) p.29. Otto Harrassowitz, 1994.)* There are several meanings to this word but to name a few; reliability, trustworthiness, loyalty, faithfulness, fidelity, integrity, honesty, confidence, deposition of trust, trusteeship etc... This amanah that we were given includes everything that Allah created for us to rely on in our worship to Him ultimately. All that we hold is actually what we hold in trust and must be used to achieve the most just ends. We are charged with creating and maintaining order in our own lives and in society. How dare we take any of it for granted! If you loaned someone your brand new car for a week and they returned it to you in a really bad condition, without any reason, you would probably feel betrayed. Wouldn't you? You sure would want to know what happened and if they would be willing to help with the damages, at least. Now when it comes to Allah you have been entrusted with your life and what was created in the Earth to rely on and to be used to gain His mercy. He does not need you to take care of these trusts but they are there as a means to the end. This end is hopefully Allah. Your journey in this life is all about getting closer to The One who created you. You are given instruction on how to keep this trust and it is an injustice to return what He has entrusted to you in perfect condition, in a manner that displeases Him. This means our physical, mental, and spiritual trusts. We will be questioned about these trusts on Yawm ul Qiyyamah(The Day of Judgement) and the proof of this is in *(The Noble Quran Surah At Takathur:8)* "Then on that day you shall most certainly be questioned about the bounties ". It is my hope that we will be able to answer in a good way bout them.

One trust that I would like to explore further and remind you and I of is our precious bodies. Our bodies do not belong to us they are entrusted to us for a specified time that only Allah knows about. We are obligated to follow the orders for maintaining them and we should seek to return to Allah with having done just that. Many of us women battle with weight almost all of our lives. We just want to be able to fit into the clothing that makes us feel good when we look in the mirror. We struggle to change our diets as we grow older and find ourselves fighting to free ourselves from the enslavement of the unhealthy foods we have been eating for so long. Many of us find it quite difficult to eat healthier foods because it just won't fit into our tight budgets. The struggle gets real tough when you begin to realize that what you ate in your 20's and kept a thin figure is not what you can eat in your 30's. Your body composition is different and if you go against that truth, you will find yourself in a constant struggle. It does not have to be this way! I encourage you to look at this whole picture in a more spiritual way!

Let's begin to ponder more on the fact that our bodies are an amanah. Let's look at it like this! The bodies that you have need tender loving care and you and I are obligated to give it just that. We have the best example of taking care of our beautiful bodies through the life of our dear beloved Prophet Muhammad, may peace and blessings be upon him. The way in which we should eat, how much we should consume and the best foods to eat as well as cures for common ailments are all laid out for us. Let's take a look at some of these examples and decide how we could incorporate them in our lives. In my opinion, it's better to take care of the inside of you first then work on the outside of you which happens almost instantly!

In the first chapter or literally the first page of the book "Healing With The Medicine Of The Prophet" *(Muhammad Ibn Aby Bakr, Ibn Qayyim Al*

Jawziyyah, and Jalal lbn Abualrab. Healing With the Medicine of the Prophet. Maktaba Dar us Salam, 2010), we find out about a few common diseases that affect the heart. The author shows proof in the Quran about these diseases as well. Among these two types are doubt and error; and lust and desire. I pondered on that chapter and wondered why it would be the first thing one should worry about. I then remembered this hadith:

On the authority of Abu 'Abdullah al-Nu'man bin Bashir (ra) who said: I heard the Messenger of Allah(sas) say:

"The halal is clear and the haram is clear, and between them are matters unclear that are unknown to most people. Whoever is wary of these unclear matters has absolved his religion and honor. And whoever indulges in them has indulged in the haram. It is like a shepherd who herds his sheep too close to preserved sanctuary, and they will eventually graze in it. Every king has a sanctuary, and the sanctuary of Allah is what He has made haram. There lies within the body a piece of flesh. If it is sound, the whole body is sound; and if it is corrupted, the whole body is corrupted. Verily this piece is the heart."

[Bukhari & Muslim]

Source: http://40hadithnawawi.com/index.php/the-hadiths/hadith-6

I would like to further explore the disease of lust and desire. If you think about it the lust and desire is what enslaves many of us more than doubt and error. We are inclined in our nature to lean towards our desires and we build a fort like structure in our hearts for them. It's like when you really desire something it becomes the thing that you cannot even take your focus off of. It's like your life depends on it and you can't live without it or even think of not having it. This is most often found in relationships. When a woman believes that she is in love with a man before marriage, she cannot stop thinking about him. She cannot eat right, sleep right, or even pray right because her thoughts have been consumed by it. The problem with this is that when the heart begins to fill up with desire of Allah's creation it has less and less room for the love of Allah. This desire for Allah's creation is now filling the heart and forces the woman to pursue it. She now goes towards marriage thinking that this will be the fulfillment of her desire and calm her heart without ever really seeking the guidance of Allah, subhanah wa ta'ala. She never prayed istikhara(prayer for guidance in a making a decision) or she prayed it once and then never paid any attention to the signs Allah may have been showing her that proved this relationship would carry her away from the love of Allah more and more. This is when the heart is in danger. It now becomes harder and harder to accept reality and one loses the protection for themselves from the delusion of a mirage. They are left empty and heartbroken if the person whom they thought they would spend the rest of their life with was not what they expected. Sometimes they remain stuck on the desire and end up remaining in marriage with this person for several months or years trying to "make it work" and then one day reality hits and they realize that it was just years of built up desires and expectations and that the relationship was not one that would lead them to the best end. That end should be Allah. It would have done them better to increase their worship of Allah and asking of His guidance and He would have guided them away from it if it was no good for their soul or toward it, making it an ease, if it were to benefit their soul. So you see this type of disease of the heart is very painful and difficult to deal with and we have to be careful with it because it invites the wrong institution of servitude. We are here to serve Allah! He has created us with everything we need upon the Earth to serve Him. The Earth was created beautifully but it is a test for us. This test is upon our conduct, how we use what is upon the Earth as a means to get closer to The Creator and attain His mercy.

(The Noble Quran Surah Al Kahf :7)

"Inna jaAAalna ma AAala alardi zeenatan laha linabluwahum ayyuhum ahsanu AAamalan"

"Verily, we have made that which is on earth an adornment for it, in order that we may test which of them are best in deeds"

- See more at:
http://www.alim.org/library/quran/ayah/compare/18/7/story-of-the-companions-of-the-cave#sthash.hlqrbLoH.dpuf

I think it is fair to say that the heart and mind must be upright in order for the rest of the body to follow in actions that are upright.

Allah does not change our condition until we change it within ourselves first.

"Verily, Allaah will not change the (good) condition of a people as long as they do not change their state (of goodness) themselves (by committing sins and by being ungrateful and disobedient to Allaah)" *[The Noble Quran Surah Al-Ra'd:11]*?.

I noticed that ever since I gave birth to my 5th child by way of cesarean section 13 years ago, I have not been the same. I was in an unhappy marriage so this just made matters worse for me both emotionally and physically. I have been battling with my weight for some time now and I know that I used to eat to avoid emotional pain. I would eat junk food like it was going out of style and whenever I went to a gathering for sisters, like during Ramadan, I would eat small meals. No one knew my battle. They all thought that I was such a picky eater and while they filled their plates full I would take my plate with small portions and eat sitting around the children, away from the adults, and when the children asked for seconds I would also help myself to seconds as well.. I just did not want to open any opportunity for the sisters to ask me a question that would force me to reveal my weakness. I never told anyone that I had a weakness with food. If any of my friends are reading this they would be shocked, to say the least, because I never showed that side of me to them. They knew that I was suffering emotionally from an unhappy marriage but I know it never crossed their mind that I was using food for comfort. I had become a slave to food! I would often stay up late at night and just eat until I felt drowsy enough to fall asleep. Then I would lie down to wake up even hungrier! I was a mess but my excuse was the emotional pain I suffered from. I had allowed it to destroy me. Whenever I was feeling emotionally bankrupt, I would get my fix from eating food uncontrollably. There was nothing anyone could tell me and in fact, no one said anything about my weight. This was quite strange to me because I knew I had gained a lot of weight since my clothes were getting smaller on me. I felt bad for myself but not bad enough to change. The feeling had become an addiction. I was addicted to feeling emotionally bankrupt because in my mind I found a "fix" and that fix was food. It was my little secret! Addiction is a serious disease no matter what the addiction is to. My addiction just happened to be food on the surface but the core revealed a lot of emotional pain. It is like taking Tylenol for a toothache but never going to the dentist to either have the tooth removed or have some other procedure done to relieve the pain permanently. I did that too actually! Many who knew me can tell you many stories about my days with toothaches. The dentist was not my friend and the Motrin given to me by the ER was good enough to relieve the pain until it got too unbearable then I would run to the dentist. I ran to the dentists because I wanted to get rid of the pain permanently. I needed to get my mouth together so that I could go back to my addiction. After getting dental work, I would go back to eating habit like every day was holiday! My husband liked to eat and I liked to cook so it all worked out. I would make full course meals and dessert almost every night of the week even when I was tired from working all day! Baking was my hobby and my kids loved that. I would make peach cobbler, pecan pies, sweet potato pies, brownies, cookies, cakes; you name it I probably made it in my kitchen! I was fascinated by food and watched the food network for hours on end on my days off with my husband and children. I really never made any of the dishes I saw I just watched it to keep my mind off of what was really going on and to have an excuse to go grocery shopping for more items, even though I spent over $400 on groceries a few days earlier. I would take forever in the supermarket too! I use to go in for one thing and walk around the entire store with that one thing then when I noticed the time that had gone by, I would start putting food items in the basket fast for fear that my husband would be upset about it. He would often ask me why I took so long as if I had gone someplace else and I gave him the excuse that I realized I needed more items. When I brought the bags inside his face would look relieved as if to say "wow I can see why you took a little longer than usual"! I was also riding the bus so that gave me more of an excuse.

I never really looked into the issue of my addiction with food until about 4 months after my divorce. I realized that when we overindulge in eating, it affects our heart. We just become enslaved by our desires totally and forget that Allah comes first and the love of Him should be deep rooted in our heart so much that when man seeks to harm or destroy us the only real and true comfort is with Him. I knew about praying Qiyyam ul Layl but I was praying and staying up later to eat more. I had not understood that I was up at a very special hour of the night and that if I truly asked with sincerity I would have gotten the comfort I needed from my Lord. I was so emotionally bankrupt and it had affected my *eeman*. I was praying those 13 rakaat (units of prayer) but it was not in asking from Allah sincerely. I just wanted to make my husband love me and do right by me but it took years for me to understand that I cannot change anyone and that I have to accept them for who they are and move on. My body was suffering and because it was entrusted to me by Allah, I was supposed to take care of it. I was destroying it because I felt that food was the only way to relieve me of the pain. I knew that Allah was in control but I had allowed the food to take control. It just sends chills down my spine thinking of what I did to myself!

It was the winter of 2012 and I felt like something about my life had to change for the better. I began thinking about how I would heal myself. Yes I am a firm believer in self- healing though I know I have to seek expert advice from the experts at times. I wanted to remove this emotional pain and so I decided to join a program run by my friend, Tahirah Taalib -Din. This was a fitness program called "Dream Body For Life" at www.dreambigandgrowrich.com. Tahirah and her husband, Antar Jannah, gave us members more than the money we invested. We got live coaching calls in the mornings and could play them all day if we missed out or wanted to repeat them, we were challenged to post our daily workouts on a private Facebook page, and we had a live feedback and check -in call on Sundays for a full hour where members would get hyped to tell their breakthrough stories and their struggles to get fit. It was so much fun and it made me feel like I was a part of a family! I did 3 cycles which were 3 months each at $1 a day and it was well worth it! I had done really well, Alhamdulilah, though I was in a major car accident the first day of the program. I did not let it stop me because I was so excited to finally find a way to shed those pounds! I went to physical therapy and made much use of the equipment there and exercised every day of the week at home. I use to walk from one town to the next tin order to go to therapy and it would take me about 90 minutes. During the last week of therapy I challenged myself to run part of the way to therapy and I succeeded! Allahu Akbar(God is Great)! My real breakthrough came when I saw that I had lost over 25 pounds then kept losing more and more each week! I felt good about myself getting on that scale and I felt like my emotions were in check finally! The sad part to it all was that it was not! I had joined this program expecting to rid myself of emotional pain but I never realized that I needed to rid of it in my mind and in my heart. My limbs would eventually follow. So after the first cycle of "Dream Body for Life" I gained back every pound I lost and found myself back at the same point from which I started. I was even 5 pounds heavier! I hated myself for allowing this to happen but it did motivate me. I mean so many good things were taking place in my life like starting my coaching business and facilitating teleseminars and coaching women in different parts of the world via internet and phone. I had been awarded a scholarship to a business school to attain my license in business coaching and began writing 2 books which I am yet to finish because of this one taking precedence since I just thought of this book only months ago! My marriage was just an unhappy place for me and I wanted nothing to do with it but I held on for another 18 months. Allah is The Best of planners!

"And if God touches thee with affliction, none can remove it but He: if He touches thee with happiness He has power over all things." *(The Noble Quran Quran 6:17)*

Recently, I have started juicing for breakfast and though the first day was hard, each day after has been getting a little bit easier. This is truly the starting point to where I have chosen to make a shift from living emotionally imprisoned and traumatized after 15 years, to living my life as if each day will be my last and with much hope in attaining Allah's mercy. I am not perfect but Allah perfectly fashioned me and I love me and no longer have to try being what someone else wants me to be. Allah is my Master! He is sufficient for all my needs! I made the goal to take charge of making my life happen on purpose on October 24, 2014- Muharram 1 1436 AH. That night I stood in Qiyyam ul Layl(The Night of Power) and asked Allah to keep me waking in the last part of the night to meet with him and help me fix what needed repairing in my life so that I could live again! Allah has, like always, kept His promise and my dua(prayer) was granted and a lot more are being granted, Alhamdulilah(All praise is due to Allah)! I have had some bumps in the road along my journey but the road seems to be leveling out. I realize that the bumps are just those areas that I need the most improvement so therefore I get tested with it more than usual.

Creating is way more difficult than maintaining but it is very necessary for change to take place. It would be to your benefit to work hard now and discipline yourselves to keep up your efforts. The body that you have been entrusted with cannot make transformation by itself. You have to put in the effort and stay the course even when the road gets rough. Put your trust in Allah if you want to really achieve victory over your battle with keeping your body upright and in good condition. Seek to serve Him and ask for His help. Believe in Yourself! Believe that it is possible! Challenge Your Weaknesses! Don't Ever Give Up!!!!

Time for A.C.T.I.O.N.

Begin with composing a P. F.A. (purpose for action) statement -

Ex: I feel good about who I am and who I am becoming. Every day is a step towards a better me. I am not defined by my past but I am who I am because God created me in this fashion. My weaknesses are present to give me opportunities for strength. I have been entrusted with this body and I know it will only benefit me in the end if I take special care of it. This is what I must do before returning to my Lord. I plan to begin my transformational journey to better health on (date)

Now compose your own using the 3 criteria below

1. Empowering positive self- statement

2. The benefit of that statement on who you would like to become or what you want to accomplish

3. Your goal

Thank You for taking the time to read "Motivated Muslimah: Permission to Win"! I am grateful and hope that you found this book to be very beneficial.

Now it's time to give yourself permission to win. Let today be the day you start taking some action to become the best version of yourself. Motivation is something that already exists inside of you and sometimes it takes work to bring it out! Are you ready? I can assist you in your journey but you, ultimately, have to do the work! We can work together to create a plan that works just for you.

Send me an email to herspiringbiz@gmail.com with "ready to win" in the subject line and I will be more than happy to spare 30 minutes of my time to discuss what you are trying to achieve. Now if you are a busy mom like myself than you know how hard it is to just get 5 minutes in the restroom without kids banging on the door right after they discover you are in there!

May Allah grant you peace within your heart, success in your endeavors, ease in your mind, ease in your heart, facilitate your difficulties, and grant you the best of health and high eemaan(faith) as you strive to take care of what He has entrusted you with-Ameen!

"Start Where You Are and Finish Where You Want to Be"~Ukhtee Walida-The Boss Moms Coach

www.ingramcontent.com/pod-product-compliance
Lightning Source LLC
Chambersburg PA
CBHW060033180426
43196CB00045B/2642